CW00551666

HIJRA

Crab Orchard Series in Poetry
Open Competition Award

HIJRA

POEMS BY HALA ALYAN

Crab Orchard Review &

Southern Illinois University Press
Carbondale

Southern Illinois University Press
www.siupress.com

Copyright © 2016 by Hala Alyan
All rights reserved
Printed in the United States of America

19 18 17 16   4 3 2 1

The Crab Orchard Series in Poetry is a joint publishing venture
of Southern Illinois University Press and *Crab Orchard Review*.
This series has been made possible by the generous support of
the Office of the President of Southern Illinois University and
the Office of the Vice Chancellor for Academic Affairs and
Provost at Southern Illinois University Carbondale.

Editor of the Crab Orchard Series in Poetry: Jon Tribble
Judge for the 2015 Open Competition Award: Cyrus Cassells

Cover illustration: "Imperial Sand Dunes" by Laurin Rinder,
cropped. *Dollar Photo Club*

Library of Congress Cataloging-in-Publication Data
Names: Alyan, Hala, 1986– author.
Title: Hijra / Hala Alyan.
Description: Carbondale : Southern Illinois University Press,
[2016] | Series: Crab Orchard Series in Poetry
Identifiers: LCCN 2016007913| ISBN 9780809335404
(softcover : acid-free paper) | ISBN 9780809335411 (ebook)
Subjects: | BISAC: POETRY / American / General.
Classification: LCC PS3601.L92 A6 2016 | DDC 811/.6—dc23
LC record available at http://lccn.loc.gov/2016007913

Printed on recycled paper. ♻

This paper meets the requirements of ANSI/NISO Z39.48-
1992 (Permanence of Paper) ∞

For Fatima Adib and Seham Abu Sharkh

CONTENTS

HIJRA

ANCESTRY

I'll lament the seeds flung
into ocean. Roots in fish gut

and everywhere the cities leak
mouths. What remains of god is

dwarfed, taken; stars expire
beneath clouds; a comet trickles

ice. All leg and eyelash, I sought
orchards torched. Our fathers tell

the story of this luminous dust,
a soil red as zinnias.

PART ONE

The exile tells himself: "If I were a bird
I would burn my wings."
Mahmoud Darwish

BEFORE THE REVOLT

We raised daughters on fog and honey.
Crickets fed us their hymns, a hook of cries—
one sapling, a half-bone, islets for neglect.
Our husbands cut steel. We suffered their bodies,
held our thighs apart like wings. At the souk,
the men sold us gold and ribbons. We built cages,
coaxed the starlings into the hour of the prophet;
moths fell from the sky in sheets,
whispering a faith fiercer than love.
When the oracle finally came to our houses,
we strung every window with chains.

NEW YEAR

I want the vandalized night, rock water
from a cavern, my eyes copper coins

strewn at the bottom of the gypsy
fountain. Owls fleck the air with

bids of love, and I am the last
of the daughters, scavenging villages

for the underfed and vicious. My wanting
cleanses me: I'm afraid, a refugee selling

flowers red as a blazing forest calls
me *wife*. We river onto maps with

shaking hands, skittish, non grata,
as the snow blankets our reckless lives.

ARIA

January

Making love in the pulsing dawn I smelled pollen
and curved like an animal. This scar is a tribute

to the hunt, blinded fish sick with oil.
We hid our breasts in the Mediterranean,

undressed only for its tongue,

carved a white kite through the night sky. Lately,
the greed of us ruins dresses and I am one

fire chasing another. Exodus will find me cutting
throats, breaking my hunger.

WEDDING

I mourn myself before you. Scattering insect
wings in the starlight. Once, I met myself
with scissors, threaded paper
across branches in lightning storms.
I sang for vessels, a hunter's moon.
To you, I give the urchin heart
of this sleeping city.

The *tamr* my prophet shook from palm trees,
fruit falling soft as styrofoam rain.
Love is the abundant pyre
assembled for gods. Darling,
you are the alarming flicker of glass in a
jade forest. The moonlight
no hands can cup.

ALCHEMY

In the tents we recite the pilfered—
queens slaughtered while dreaming of coves,
the ossuaries
      beneath the Mediterranean.

When an animal dies
we fill the soil with apologies and shells,
      climb the sloping dunes
where gods were offered headless men.

Lanterns stipple the altar with shadows,
one body birthing another.
      At night we cry out *suras* and cover the grass
with our hair. Beauty will survive us:

hyacinth motes atop ruins,
all of paradise trembling legs, the delicate mess
of ligaments,
      teeth, and jaw.

THE CHILDREN

Carried on our backs through desert,
      heliocentric objects with open mouths.
We taught them to love the ugly sky,
      chiseled their bodies into pale legs, teeth
that tilled milk from our breasts until
      nothing was left but water and blood.
Mercy, we cried for snakemouth orchids,
      illustrations of a kingdom without gods.
Because there was no money,
      we tatted lace from the sea, scraped honey
from nests. We befriended the wealthy
      in villas and scrubbed their bathtubs.
It didn't matter who loved the flute,
      the furs, the garnet necklace. We stole it all.

INVASION

Was it not September choking
down thunder and hail,
eating away at the cast-iron
statues until even the wings
melted into some creature
flooded and featherless,
a skyline of crackling red trees

Was it not footfall that came through
the roofs of river houses,
floorboards beneath wolves
howling flight, saying hide
the girls for God's sake;
they're coming and they're starved

Everywhere sulfur rises, crocuses explode,
lovers walk in pecan groves
and smell rust, rows of oleander
within the monsoon

Each gold finch
unhooks her song at dusk,
as militias gather lungs

MARRIAGE

The men burnt flags and draped shrouds
in their place. They marshaled the spirits of the

village, pulsing in little jugs atop the mantle.
We dressed like stones for them, gray, submerged,

ready to be pitched. Every evening we rinsed
their feet with dark water bowls, steadied them

for Allah. The night folded into their skin—
freckles from where the dead kissed them.

When they dreamt of horses in the river, a sky
with thunder for drowned animals galloped,

we watched the fever dew their foreheads and pled
for ice. Even the white dawn couldn't make

the men smile, and so we split ourselves for them.
We forgave the love that coiled in their fists.

RAPTURE IN ABSENTIA

You found him in the riverbank, his mouth
filled with silt. Damp soil, damp hair,

birds making a hole of his abdomen,
and nothing left to love in that land.

You lit fires, built a ship of nettles,
and sailed into a starless month.

In the new city, rich women love
like dark bruises of rotting fruit.

They ash themselves into unfamiliar beds.
You ate cacti, spines and all,

became a lighthouse for sharks.
You carve his name with their teeth.

THE YOUNGEST WIFE

While the village celebrated the war
      with firecrackers and roses,
dancing around a charred flag,
she planted azalea bulbs

in crevices of razed soil,
      crooning under a blank sky.
Of the garden we knew only plunder.
Unpinning things by their necks.

In beauty, aching becomes a
      triumph. After, we placed
her bones inside a circle of thistle,
spilled mounds of salt at the four

corners of the pillaged garden.
      We migrated like legless birds
from one man to the other,
eating the pollen in their beards.

HIJRA

Sleepwalkers, uterus dust, you heard the gunfire

and folded into clay. We begged our bodies for
alchemy, death into new lungs; we fed bread

to the *jinn*. The clouds followed us, a scrap
of summer moon as gazelles made a meal of ash.

We became seamstresses, mapping departure
into our eyelids. Allah's calligraphy stitched

our vertebrae. We wrote their unsaid names
on parchment, buried them in boxes, gave birth

to our daughters in caves. When our breasts wept
milk for months, we drank it ourselves.

THE PROPHECY

You will wait two moons for the burning to end.

When geese begin to feast on the eyes, one cobbled road
will turn to smoke,

      and you will catch crows with white beaks that fall

from their skulls and dot the coastline with tents.

      Without this land you will become a drought, a musk
of scorched bread will trail you aboard boats.

Your mouth will become a tin cup.
In the city of glass, you will harvest fog.

PART TWO

In the deluge on our plains there are no rains but stones.

Etel Adnan

BUDUR

The perished city arrives on postcards:
I carry the shale, the pyres are coming.
We follow one another from island
to river, etch the names of dead men
onto our necks with the smoldering tip
of sparrow feathers, as distant towers
tumble with smoke. Green and azure,
the bright embers flare and vanish
into water. Sisters, this is redemption—
a man setting himself on fire inside
the mosque, a rooftop of white fronds,
throats choking on forgotten names.

AZRA

There is a tunnel, elsewhere, that I live in.
It is a house full of nails and not one hammer.

By midmorning cicadas narrate testaments.
I name my daughters after the fled villages,

Akka, Qira. They speak the language of falcons,
lyrics about animal hearts, succulent,

red. They awaken the mice with their dreaming.
If there is a husband, he salts the soil.

Nothing is merciful with him, and when he sings
I see twenty women tearing satin dresses,

black finches swarming the coast.
He says I have hands like Baghdad.

I wonder if he means the tending or the torching.

KHADIJA

Before the drought, it was a white dress. Fingers tipped in henna,
red as the chest of a hummingbird,

hair like a banyan tree. Even in this strange city, fruit dusts itself
with spores. I am a dirt toward which rain rushes,

garlanding, your body dusky with the exile of sleep.
We practice a new alphabet. Love,

they say the bullets are filling the streets we danced in.
They say the lucky are dead.

SEHAM

Sit and I'll tell you of my father's prayer rug,
dark as plums with yellow borders,

borders like the map we ate, grit tangled
between our teeth, the years swelling

like one hundred arrows. Here,
have some stew, taste June in the steam.

Did I tell you about the name we bore
like armor, the earth they spat up

with fishbone? After they planted copper
in our eyes, we went on planting suns over

the graves. The air smelled of
burning clementine groves. We fed

our daughters until they grew
redwoods and oak trees instead of hearts,

the fever we took from the land when
our ribs turned into compasses.

MAYSAM

A mantle of charcoal and soot
wets the villages like cigars.
The elders swung white
from tree branches but us daughters
excavated romances
from the debris. We adored
the soldiers with their pale
hair. They ordered our grandfathers
to open satchels, and we pinched
our cheeks for color. Their rifles
hung like jewelry. When the luckiest
of us were given heels of bread
by the soldiers, we laughed and
danced. We batted away the elders'
warnings: *Don't eat that bread.*
What could those ancient
women with wrung breasts and
ugly legs know of reckoning?
New flags shot up like flames,
and we kissed the soldiers' lips,
tasted ash and honey.

LUJAYN

After we buried our men,
no rain fell for twelve moons,
a eulogy of famine. Dust covered
the rows of effigies, and we slit
oysters open for their sea.
When a dove flew into the tent,
she carried a warning in her larynx,
of the hunger, the apostates of love
we would discover in our bodies,
psalms like unopened eggs in the
nests of our lungs. We hunted the
marshes and dry valleys, the bazaars
of Eid, sitars and metal necklaces,
mangoes and ropes of garlic.

HADEEL

Falcons follow wrens
inland—
     a coastline
     of wing tips

Algae drifting in emerald braids
one of my sister's braids

What endures of any lament is penance
or relapse—
     a man's tibia
     bare feet
     upon stone

a body in pieces at the mosque

     hair smelling of coriander
     in the hands—

REEMA

Pillow talk,
a driveway of rime
salted, the you
you broke in your
father's Ethiopia.
Tonight the tide,
the nightly sigh.
I remember how
I clutched the
books, how a man
stopped us at
the border and
made us undress
beneath the glare
of a headlight,
how he left us
in the birches,
cupping what was
once inside us,
and no longer is.

ZAYNAB

A lighthouse, a false sun on the sand.
We borrowed oceans for wakes and retrieval.
We left a pale sea behind,
almond trees, hawks, a year of blown skies.
Marketplaces full of tusks and guavas,
the moons men broke into our bodies for.

On the sand, a trio of dogs snarls,
feeds on a pelican carcass, sinews glistening;
we yell at them, bang spoons on metal cans.
The light shines wet before the sea takes it.

YASMIN

Each dark is an unburied doll clasped in shaking hands.

O flesh, a comet speckling the night

as the men cried out *repent, repent,*
and I ate grain the rats ate.

For three days, I wept as fire crowned my feet and ears,
La ilaha illAllah

A storm was leaping on treetops—

I saw a house after the plague.
August had caked the windows with sand.

Inside, bodies dangled from the ceiling like swans.

LAMIS

The stables are
flooded. Cupful
of earth, half
a century searching.
We ate the goats
where they bled.
Aleppo-bound
I've made a shy
mossy bed of salt.
Pebbles. Jasmine tea.
I'll buy you an ocean,
was the last thing
you said to me before
the trees fell and
by sundown they had
come to take you.

AMNA

In the eucalyptus forest we cut eyes

into bark, watched smoke
eclipse sun after sun. After dark,

crickets recited requiems, *ya ummi,*
ya abi; we roasted pigeons

over fires for the children.
Forgive us the eating, the red

desire of our bodies, this grief
that blisters us, and we pop

into mercy. Love is filching
your child's air from her white throat,

feeding her to the river before
the army arrives. Ask any woman.

Love is what kicks and kicks
beneath your steady hand.

SANA

It was green as moss, the mist I parted
to find sea glass in the Andalusian sand.
The water, a dim chant to the stars.
With jewels in each ear I shone
like a candle, one of those wistful
women who set out bowls of rice for
the dead. Now, I break light on sundials,
gather the purple corpse of each hour
as stars chase one another like swallows.

FATIMA

The birds have a different aubade here,
of revival and dominion.
Along the Midwest, a hallucination
of highway light after light as signs blur by.
A tundra of strip malls and bankrupt towns.

On the prairie, the horses appear in a startled rush,
blotting the hills with silken brown bodies.
Amrika is the pink meat we fry in oil to crisps.
My daughters grow fleshy and cunning.

They speak of barbarity like a hope,
fat stars anchored in lanterns for Allah to see.
The cold twists my bones into a nest,
and the window becomes a creek of fingers.

AFRA

Dear S.,

They're burning tanks again.
In the airport custody room, they asked me
where I came from and I said yes.
I let them open my suitcase, rifle through
the skirts and sandals, that pillbox
your mother left me. No, I said nothing
when they asked of you, wanting to know
about Mosul and the seven afterlives,
I only said you were dead. Aren't you?
(In Tigris, a rumor. In Istanbul, gospel.)
I never asked you, how could you bear it?
The shepherding and return, loving a man
everyone wanted to see slain.
I know what you'll say. That I'm flimsy,
of girlish stock. (You never forgave how
I set those geese free.) But you're wrong.
I can recite you every word Cain told Abel.
(Come home, *habibi*. I never said I'm sorry
and I am.) I kept the stones you left me.
You've no idea what a temple I built.

PART THREE

The map must be of sand and can't be read by ordinary light.

Joy Harjo

MEALS

In the beginning, we ate oceans,
        translucent oysters, fish eggs, a radiant orb

of green,
licked the brine off our fingertips.

*

        Cassiopeia tosses her eyes over our
feast of sand and milkweed.

We emerge from the dawn like *jinn,*

        catch wind and drizzle with aluminum bowls.

*

A thousand empty hands.

The children clasp at each living thing—
        beetles and crunchy moth wings.

They suck the dirty ice.

*

        The plate is a black eye, winter berries buried
in a cup of sand.

We eat the gazelle tongue first.

Her language engulfs us: grass pastures, sky,
mushroom clusters

budding in the field of poinsettias.

*

The men steal clams from the market.

Savage longing, our mouths fill
with the spines of creatures slow enough to catch.

ASYLUM

They said burn the keys
but only our hair caught fire.

We walked to the borders
with photographs and letters:
this is where the dying began
their dying, this is where
they knifed the children.

The judges called us in
by our cities. Jericho. Latakia. Haditha.

We swore on a god we never met, to love
the lakes, the ice caps,
one frost after another,

but at night in our dreams
the library burnt,
the pears were still crisp in the pantry.

We waited for our flooded village
to be siphoned, the stone bridges rebuilt.
We ate the house keys with salt.

FIRST WINTER

Our bodies are urns full of rain. The elders
speak of clemency. The army marches on.

We watch them across the ocean,
speak their undead names in our sleep.

Some of the sisters still make mosques
out of straw in abandoned lots. They wake

to Allah's ninety-nine names, while
the neighborhood boys hawk the spires

for cocaine. In the hour of the blizzard,
the devout speak of owls rising from

fossils. When they bathe, they hear
voices swelling in the pipes, open their

mouths wide to catch their wombs
brimming with thirst. They name

the trees in the projects for Hagar.
Snow fills the minaret, and they wait

to arrive, at last, blinking, to God.

PLUMAGE

April

The island bursts with silver birches, puffs
of chrysanthemum swept open. *Habibi,*

in the dream your voice rises, singing of the
aviary where we arched like dusklight

over stone, ajar, amazed with breaking.
Habibi, they flayed you, cut rope

for your cellist fingers. Only the women
make a husk of this grief. We hang X-rays

from our new windows, let the sun
toss our bones across the walls.

IN THE CITY OF FIRE

The years pass. We leave the wreckage for the birds
and live in skyscrapers now,
hang paintings of glaciers midthaw.

When the city meets her tombs,
we pour whiskey into tumblers and sigh. We say
this country makes you hard. Even the dead starve.

The mothers march parades through the cemetery.
Joy is for the afterlife, they say,
and drape the headstones with myrrh and lace.

The keys hang between the breasts of our daughters now.
They palm cigarettes and speak of revolution.

We tell them the prophets have been dead for ages,
the flags crumbled in the riots.

Our hands fill like volcanos at the dying cities,
but we tore the atlas into psalms.

In our houses, we leave every lightbulb burning,
keep the music cranked up loud and fast
for the god we will never let sleep.

IDOLS

It is easy to love the
bridges, their spider

legs black and divine
between two filthy coasts.

They are alive.
The ambulances

spill their crimson
light over the water,

Allah's long neck
tipped back to drink rum.

There is not a single
pomegranate in this

land, but when dawn
carves itself on trees,

it's enough to make you
tunnel across the sea,

the thousands who died
smelling apples in the air.

THE LETTER HOME

Tell her of the bronzed children. Your son's home spinning with laughter, their voices delicious even if you cannot understand the words the youngest uses to describe the waves. At night, they gather around the flame of the television and eat cakes sprinkled with sugar. On the night of the comets, the youngest takes you outside, says follow the tail and the sky bursts violet. His Arabic is rusty, and you teach him the word for *clementine* as you watch the fire above. Tell her of the curtain of bees that covers the largest ash tree in your son's backyard and how he says his name all wrong in this country, like someone has cleared his mouth of bells. Your mouth is full of bells, and no one seems to hear when you ask for rosewater to rinse sinks with. They dance to maracas here, and none of the children whimper when thunder comes. Tell her of the other night, when your son took you to the lighthouse and you stood stunned, watching the light dapple the water soft as an unwrinkled green sheet. Tell her you are afraid of the supermarket, the bright displays, the girl who bags your oranges without saying a word. Tell her you miss your city like a lung. You miss the crakes, the fickle sea washing along driftwood, the way even the locusts bring music, tell her you wake at dawn weeping for figs, and when she writes back she will call you a fool, she will say sister, sister, they've turned this land into a grave.

ASKING FOR THE DAUGHTER

Because she stood palm-first to the sky. A raindrop,
then a dozen more. Because she is climbing tombs

with those legs of fire, stone houses to lace the gray
cypress with sunlight. Because she eats fruit with

dirt and lime salt. Everywhere the mud blossoms.
Because she can name each of the wrecked temples.

Because moon. Because ruin. Because a woman
who knows war knows deliverance, her mouth a sea

of sharks trapped in coral. Because she broke
into the flooded shopping mall and played cello in

the wet atrium. There was no one inside.
Even the security guard pretended not to hear.

RETRIEVAL

Rapture in tunnels, in that radiant fever
of black dahlias flinging their sex
into the heavy air, gods and their wild-eyed
saints, a sea that whips itself into a
plunging dark. From the shipwreck they pulled

pyrite, instruments that shroud their
lost music. Rapture in chalky stars slung into
the ribcages of magnolia trees, windows mottled
milky with children diving for bottles. O grief,
when the owls begin their slow, gentle croon,
may we climb onto the highest pillar and
gather ourselves for the first wind like mammals.

DIASPORA

A man with gnarled hands
plucks the tiny beaded eyes
of an octopus gray and braised

on a bed of ice. Your village fell
fifty years ago, arched like an arrow
and scattered. Iridescent scales

cling to his fingertips in
rainbow glints. Electric with ruin,
the villagers learned their way

through rubble. They named each
sinking house for a lunatic god.
The man wraps the fish in twine

and brown paper. When it was over,
children littered the bridge.
There was no one left to grieve.

PART FOUR

I wanted to be those stairs, the hunger I felt, the river inside.

Kazim Ali

FOLIAGE

Meimei, what Damascus road ran vermillion and dusty as you waited for your father. What girlhood did you find nestled in the potted plants on the balcony. Tulips begin to shake their tongues like slippers. Wing tips, calyx. Your voice catches.

The flower is its own organ.

I took your favorite scarf and wrapped it around my head. *Insh'Allah, ya rab.* Faith dipped into my hand like a wren, dull and timid. Even in exit I married my false name, repeated its dark miracle to men. I turned with the foliage. Cartographer's delight: the damp umbrella, a sable evening gown, the hairpins and matchsticks rattling inside the kitchen drawer.

Balding trees line the road, frothed with kidney-red flowers, a spring of repair undone. You barely remember me anymore. My sister and I look too much alike; your sons are busy with wives. Love is an arrival, Meimei, it is the damask tablecloth you pile with *kousa* and lamb, the porcelain saucer of pumpkin seeds I suck salt from. The hand you plunge into a fern's soil.

Binti, *the root is the last to die.*

In America, I say my grandmother is ill, I say there is a blankness feathering her, that she fills teacups and believes her father is waiting for her in Syria, furious that she missed the last rickety bus home. Beyond the bars smelling of yeast, dusk drops its mink across the city.

HAMRA

When the bombing begins, we move the long yellow couches away from the windows and pour arak into glasses. The road that leads east cuts beneath the balcony, calls of one man to another audible below. They are saying the morning belongs to the obedient. I am braless, half-asleep, trying to listen to the newscaster describe the explosion, her slender hands flitting like earnest birds diving for fish.

My friend is undressing and, between swigs of arak, she cries out for the war to eat her lover. My arteries are ugly, she moans. He scooped me bare.

The road that leads east cuts beneath the balcony, and a spidery cloak of stars above. This is a time of fear, we are told. On the telephone, my father's voice crinkles and falls, tells me to lock the doors. But they are already inside, I want to say. The men are in the living room, they have eaten the last of the plums. Atop the stove, the soup is burnt to a crisp, only a blackish scent remains. We'll bring you nettles, the men say.

My friend's lover arrives with rope. On the street, one of the men is shot, and we listen to him bleed, all the while cursing the brother that left him for America. The sun thieves through the curtains, bleached ivy.

It has taken decades for this city to die, the newscaster says. Her own house has been swallowed by sea, and she shakes sand from her collarbone on air. Years ago, my father owned a window in Oklahoma, then Texas, then the dry summers whittled his accent and he never returned. I tell the story to my friend and her lover, and they pour me another glass.

The road that leads east is cut, glass covering asphalt like shredded paper. There is a sharp odor: snapped telephone wires. We lend the neighbors our balcony, point out the men picking their teeth and laughing. See, we say. The earth has changed only for the extinct.

The electricity is out and in the hours before sunrise, we drink and talk about films. Another round of gunshots, a woman screams her daughter's name. I used to think trees lived on the bottom of the ocean, the lover says. Not coral reef, kelp, but cottonwoods and elms, women with magenta hair planting onion bulbs into the seabed. We mock him. What about spores, we ask, what about oxygen and loam?

He shrugs. Even without sunlight they would bloom.

MARROW

Three men argue from the veranda:
He feeds me like a highway. A foghorn
    of awful dinners. The Bethlehem rain,
long and slow. Animals stole from
    tea bitter with clove. I am drunk again
mugs. *Corazon,* he says. By September,
    in the dream, they are eating phosphorus.
We had scoured the beaches:
    The world is. Even Yarmouk sings,
found amongst pines a lonely way to love,
    Beirut: the cafés are exploded,
my narcotic rent. The five doors
    panes of magnified glass, warlit—
inside my wilder body awaiting
    the sexy eyes of the latest martyr,
his sly footsteps. Bonfire,
    shrapnel kissed to his forehead
your questions crowding—
    this midnight breeds in me doubt.
Who had you. With what marrow.
    A guard translated for me the question:
Finding the church to say I'm sorry,
    what would you prefer, land or exit?
I dreamt him in Peru. Afghanistan.
    One orphans, the other frees.

SALAT

When I asked *regrets?* you could speak only of the cement rooftops
the woman you left for Arizona

who took thirty-two Ativans and drove herself to your father's house

You give what you give to reclaim it

*

The fog a necklace around the bridge

I am possessed as in possessed by the sound of checkpoint guards
     whistling;
they love tap the taxi's windshield

the joke of *how many Beirut girls does it take*

*

In Girona we climb marble stairs
to find an unwashed couple sleeping in the grass

Ramadan, *baba*, I fast for the plastic tarps, hypothermic infants,
     ebola winter,

my grandfathers' names—Salim, Mohammad—

*

For the afternoon tea, we gather in the elders' parlors,
kissing their fingertips

introducing ourselves hurriedly—somewhere, a film reel unspools—

ibn Fares, *bint* Hilal, we recognize ourselves by what we belong to

MANIA

She doesn't feed the carp anymore, the bathtub brassy with algae. When the children pull kudzu from the ground, she scolds them. *We are meant to take very little,* she says, and her voice trembles with the heft of February, her fervor to feel a body crooked over hers, the little alphabet she uses her forefinger to trace inside her thighs. She wishes to be a woman on yesterday's wall, gone and retrieved, her hair a hundred blackbirds midflight.

Absence makes worshippers of the feral, she says. Her body is the punctured tin, love the unlucky geraniums. Meanwhile, moths. A circlet of ovens unshut. Standing above a hill, she counts antlers, bellowing for the coyotes to hear.

Here is the orbit, they answer. Here are the seven ways of ablution, of shaping cellars from a moist dirt.

Flashlit, last sister in a ladder of asps. The helicopters are dropping fire, she says. I am a cocktail dress rusting from smog and lightbulbs. The madness of a headlamp swaying in oil tunnels.

When she names god, beneath the moon-sodden shrubs, something flickers beneath her chest, an unkempt meteor, a domestic tree that she chops into pieces and forgets to water in her dreams.

BANDITS

You were mama's: first and only boy, sable eyelashes long as an ostrich. Operatic, I claimed *baba*, his books and his sulk, first of the unrequited loves. What we took we took unasked.

Between us, staticky, fast, our song on the radio during the war.

Brother, I know your smoke, your quiet, how we disobeyed everyone by staying out, red-eyed, cajoling the jukebox *one more, one more* on a bad dollar. The wine I drank found its way to your stomach. When you fevered I burnt.

Archeologists, sifting the frame of twenty-six houses, half a dozen countries, the Arabic that'll never belong to us. One long laundry list we commit to memory only to forget again, calling each other from American coasts at midnight with urgent questions: *ghadab* is *feda'* is *thawra*.

On trips home, we filled cheap suitcases with Persian silk, jars of pickled olives, translated Qurans.

No grandmothers left to stop us.

SCRIPTS

But first, the mimicry of lyrebirds.
The crescent moon, that brook

making pianos of the rocks.
A homeless woman holding spoons

in her blackened fingers, telling you
they took the city and wore her blood.

You, uneasy, offering
to buy her milk, stamps, ma'am,

I'll miss the bus. After the reading,
a man asks about your addict,

the *catlike whirring* of your words,
his own garbled with vermouth:

you, in lace-up boots, you,
twelve pirouettes at a nightclub,

disco lights blue as jacaranda
against your perspiring skin.

Outside, a cloudless night,
a sky so listless it scripts egrets

into a swoop of gray. We have
left this place to the birds, left them

our uneaten apple seeds, the flashing
skeleton of a neon sign,

the partygoers talking about
the latest beheading,

your friend's friend, *an amazing guy*,
his eyes aloof and blue on the

laptop screen because *don't look away*,
because *those fucking animals*,

the worship of the tree is what
cleaves it. Beneath the neon, *I must, I must.*

SOLARIUM

You trusted only what undid you—metal fences, the key thrown
back into the swimming pool. Your hips split by a man you did not
love. The switchblade, bright and unholy in your purse. On the
third month, you walked down a hallway in the hospital gown—a
snow of crushed pills—shadows knotting into nails.

This is not your husband, not your uninvited muscle, the scuttle of
insect voices emerging from the river's edge. I loved your sneakers,
your awning, the dark braid you lost to a man with scissors. You
grew, north; you weeded the heart of its seeds. Look, I made a
valentine for us: the city throbbing like a voltage, those anchors
flared into a tow of tiny boats. Between summers, you turned a man
into greenhouse, larch slit for sap, wooden urns brimming with
kernels and sea glass.

Life gathers the living like flies: you loved Ovid's gods, the doomed
brides and warriors parting golden fields. More than life you wanted
fear, alleyways to dart through, a rag soaked with kerosene and held
above your head. Beyond you, smashed cars. Your malty breath.
Sirens. The ribbon that held her black ponytail up. Yours is the rose
the luna moths ate into our winter blankets.

The rocks around your ankle, your voice bitter—*I'll haunt for
it*—through the emergency rooms, the tossed fluorescent lights,
dirty sinks of tinfoil and spoons. This was not my body, your voice
not the wet shell against my ear. This was the good-bye spoken in
three languages. I left you in that bar, arm snaked around your
own waistline as you nodded. Ten years later, I kept the newspaper
photograph of you dancing in a solarium, to a ferocious music I
could no longer hear.

EXILE NOCTURNE

I

A feeding of light. Myself, dumb, in the lap of a lent man. Every morning a gin. Every morning an engine. Heave of flowerpot against the wall, unelectric hurricane. We toast to the tourists, tracking Phoenician dirt onto linoleum floors. Romantic meat, moonward.

II

A decade has passed. No longer the arcades, our noontime traffic, a needle arrowing the hollow of typewriter. The men licking nipples like stamps. What one covets the other breaks. Up or down, I turned their names loose through the trees, nailed the letters to a doorway. It was not courage that made me leave but defeat.

Pickups followed me home. My coyote body bent and narrow, tiny wilts, singing myself to the junkyards, the revolver still warm in his boot.

On the last day of November, I poured wax into plates, held my breast against the hardening.

III

The row of turquoise sparklers, milk crates, I spout beneath the spires, gilded and fragile. I am July, flattened out by drought, houseless as a mollusk arched in two.

No one touches me for months, I'm thrumming with it, pure as a single marigold inside a wineglass kept by a poisoned girl. Through the blackout, I walked the smoke trees of Harlem. I slept until afternoon. I woke to find my leg bleeding, the curtains missing. His photograph in each room of that house; I was the hallelujah forced from tongue.

Voodoo like the inside of a sycamore. The fire hydrants coated with snow.

A ring for every finger.

RIOTS

In the dream you are saying *conch*.

I tell you your betrayal saved me. It was the pickax that struck gold,
Orpheus in reverse. I say the men that smelt of varnish have gone.
You were my Basra, I say, my Tripoli, the house catching my silences
with slackened jaw. I'll bring back the tequila, my bleached hair
tipped with blue. I'll bring every flask I drank, my mouth sweeping
against yours. You smoke those terrible Lucky Strikes and ask the
women to cut your hair.

I'm the ghost that never dies, you joke. Suddenly, we are walking
down that street of bars and cafés, the men patrolling with rifles.
The jade leaves of the trees shimmer like sliced iridium. Beneath
every opaque thing is something pliant, an eyeless kiln. You tell me
the hydrangeas died after I left; silverfish burrowed in the eaves.

I play a game sometimes, I tell you. I go back to that night and ask
myself what to leave, what to take. There is always a man yelling, a
clock counting down. Photographs. Laptop. Ring. You or me?

TRANSATLANTIC

Z, I'll meet you as dawn
splinters the city into
a forest of reed and lichen.
Remember us lost.
Remember us before this
longing, asleep in
each of our houses—
yours ancient, mine lush
with the scent of rosemary,
irises zippered between
fallen mosques. Each rainfall
incites the paradise
you spoke of, unworn rubies,
carafes of silk, a glorious sky.
You are the leopard and the
beautiful prey it stalks,
mouth poised over a pool
of melted snow. I wanted
silver mist, a veil of
wasps thronging the lilies, pink
grapefruits pulped and
nested with ants. I wanted
abandon. You held
the slender neck of the viola,
wrote verses about birds
and their skulls.
Trees are the ships that
house us now. Our lives lit.
You say exodus will save us,
a necklace of grungy cities.
I'll do *wudu* a thousand times.
I'll pray to your scientific god.

CHIROPHOBIA

Today I watched a woman bleed, scarlet thumbprints from her lip,
speckling the collar of her blouse. She flicked her eyes—cactus
green, refugee green—toward the window and said, *Forgive
me*. I washed her hands, the sandalwood soap slim and uneven,
moistened the tip of a towel to wipe across her face. First she spoke
in Arabic, then in a language I'd never heard before, syllables gutted
as she spoke of silhouetted hillsides and sundials, tides shedding into
granite. I remembered the Mayan temples of Tulum as she spoke,
the way I pretended the ocean crashing below the cliff was the
thousand bare feet of men rushing to plunder. The cenotes, jagged
stalagmites in the shape of buried cities, my fiancé's fingertips
tugging the elastic of my bikini hipline while saltwater clogged our
ears. The woman told of playing a harp many years ago, in the plush
rooms of a restaurant in her village, a place the wealthy flocked
in their diamonds and silk ties. The men applauded her, and after
the final drink was raised, she always unknotted her hair slowly,
heard the sighs as curls fell down her shoulders like a black flood.
In the evenings, walking home along the only road, she pulled
ragweed to boil. She married the first man who filled her glass with
champagne. He stacked her wrists with gold. They moved to an
ornate house in a border town, rooms long and saffron as vases. In
the winter, she would dream of metallic hands holding scales and
wake in the garden, nightgown clinging to her legs. Here the story
ended, and the woman began to wail, grabbing fistfuls of her hair
and yanking toward the ceiling, floor, the gentle spring outside the
clinic walls. She was drunk, and swaying, and I was frightened—for
her, of her, of a love so rotten it mends, of the woman I have always
suspected lives beneath my thrifty anatomy: alive, urban. Attic in
a flesh of salt and wine. Back at home, I composed letters, then fed
them one by one to the bathwater. *Dear, I once crushed a viola to the
ground. Dear, I am a cell beneath a sunless eye. Afraid to touch, and
more afraid not to.*

FORECASTING

For J

Come winter—silver ponds, telescopes, the firecrackers of midnight.
A heart that fishtails itself broken, ethereal ventricles and the aorta
slick with blood. Urgent, pesky. The body is transparent in its
wanting, amulets diagrammed easily on the inside of a palm—a
cedar pronged into branches of need, the rivers sewn and precise in
their ending—always, it's rudderless, a lithograph for departure.

I am the yes, yes, mushrooming from a plucked thorax, the rack
of good, salty lamb I will never cook you, the plot of sundews in
another wife's lawn. Admire the architecture of my moving chest,
the delirium of my wrists, how you come like an ocean receded and
then returned, lit by rain and acid. The father who made me risky so
men would beg for it. For the forest that one becomes searching for
origin, carrying the seedpods and nighthawks, the thyme and Xanax
of mama's cupboard, the card deck I split in half for spite. It is true—
in the bistro the coffee dregs skittered into elk, canoes, aerial limbs
speaking the amen of a late marriage.

You dream of August, a dozen fluted stems unfurled into
candelabra. Everywhere, berries drop like purple snow; unfallen
storms husk the air. I dream the same dream, only the rain has
come and gone, laundering the trees to alabaster bark. My lungs are
grass. They find a wind and call for you.

LIONS

The country on the map was teal, fat and jutted, large as an open palm striking flesh. It was a bulky jag of land between two navels of water, a tangled gulf. The mother considered it an afterthought, miles of convenience and amnesia, someplace to birth her eldest and hold her tiny lolling head up for photographs. On the airplane back, the mother kept stealing touches into her purse, fingering the stiff rectangle of the passport, pleased as a pickpocket. She thought of how the doctor had pronounced her daughter's name, the gleaming stethoscope around his neck. Once home, she flung windows open, the desert air still, shaking her head with mock exasperation at the thin layer of dust that found even the cleanest drawer. She quickly forgot the country, though sometimes she dreamt of a papery hospital gown, the sound of larks. She never spoke of those dreams, only the one of lions walking the highways and marketplace of her hometown, gnawing upon the palm trees with yellow teeth. When the army burst through the city walls, the mother was still sneaking bites of her daughter's fourth birthday cake. Her belly swelled with a heartbeat. Tanks slashed through bronze gates, clouds torn by bitterns. Tinsel scraps and streamers still clung to the cream-colored walls. It was August, rows and rows of fires lit in the dunes. The mother got into a car and drove east, past the fumes and gunfire, in a line of cars snaking across the desert, quickening, the sun rising and setting claret. Smoke trailed above them like buzzards, the spatulas the mother left behind, the armoires and crystal bowls, her own husband left in the ambushed city. On the side of the road, she fed her daughter ice streaked with filth and ants, then held her head as she vomited. When she reached her grandfather's town, the mother fell to the courtyard tiles and prayed, for the two heartbeats inside her, for her daughter's fever, for the husband who would return to her emptied. Years later, the daughter would remember the oil-stained tablecloth of those evenings, her mother speaking the lion tongue. When they arrived in the teal country months later, the mother peered outside the airplane window as they circled cornfields, watched the land come closer, tufts of tall grass rustling with wind, a stripe of road etched into the pastures. In their new home, men howled outside the window, beer bottles glittered on the tracks. The mother spoke to the heartbeat of this place, the sepia winter that arrived abruptly, as though a blanket of wool was pitched over the squat apartment complexes, the frog skeleton she found in the parking lot one morning, how she wept at the departing Vs of birds. Of the women that sat drinking on the compound stairs like fallen deities, and how the mother kept her eyes on the mound of her belly as she walked. The heartbeat glimmered. After the first snow came and melted, the mother walked outside in the early light, wearing only a thin cotton robe, the bottles dotting a murky green on the concrete, walked the compounds until her toes went numb, past the gas station and park, back into the cramped apartment where everyone slept, and knelt in front of the makeshift vault beneath the thin mattress. She pulled the blue passport into the air, she cursed it and cursed it and raised it to her lips.

ACKNOWLEDGMENTS

Grateful acknowledgment is made to the editors of the journals below, where the following poems appear:

Blackbird: "In the City of Fire" and "Retrieval"
Colorado Review: "Hijra" and "Transatlantic"
Columbia Poetry Review: "Azra" and "Rapture in Absentia"
Diode: "Alchemy," "Khadija," "The Letter Home,"
    "Maysam," and "New Year"
Four Way Review: "First Winter"
Guernica: "Asylum"
Harvard Review: "Afra"
Missouri Review: "Meals"
Mizna: "Forecasting"
Prairie Schooner: "Marriage" and "Plumage"
Split This Rock: "Bandits"

A huge thank you to Cyrus Cassells for selecting my work, and to Jon Tribble and Southern Illinois University Press for bringing my work to life. I am indebted (always) to the time and encouragement of Fady Joudah.

Thanks to my lovely husband Johnny for the support and inspiration: you've consistently made room in our little apartment for my writing, and for that I adore you. I am grateful for Talal, without whom I wouldn't have known how to begin (again). For Salim Salem, who taught me that books are just as important to love as people. Thank you to the friends and family (Baba, Mama, Miriam, Reem, Layal, Omar, Atheer, Dalea, Sarah, Kiki, Michael) whose patience and love I'm lucky enough to have, even if I don't always deserve it. Thank you to my grandmothers for showing me the thousand ways to be a strong woman. Meimei, you made me in your image and I hope you'd be proud of me today.

Finally, thank you to the women that came before me, and to the women that will come after.

OTHER BOOKS IN THE CRAB ORCHARD SERIES IN POETRY